Adult Coloring Book of Animals

Relax with this Calming, Stress Managment, Animal Colouring Book for Adults

Grahame David Garlick

www.southshorepublications.com

Copyright © 2015 SouthShore Publications

ISBN-13: 978-1517529147

ISBN-10: 151752914X

LIONESS

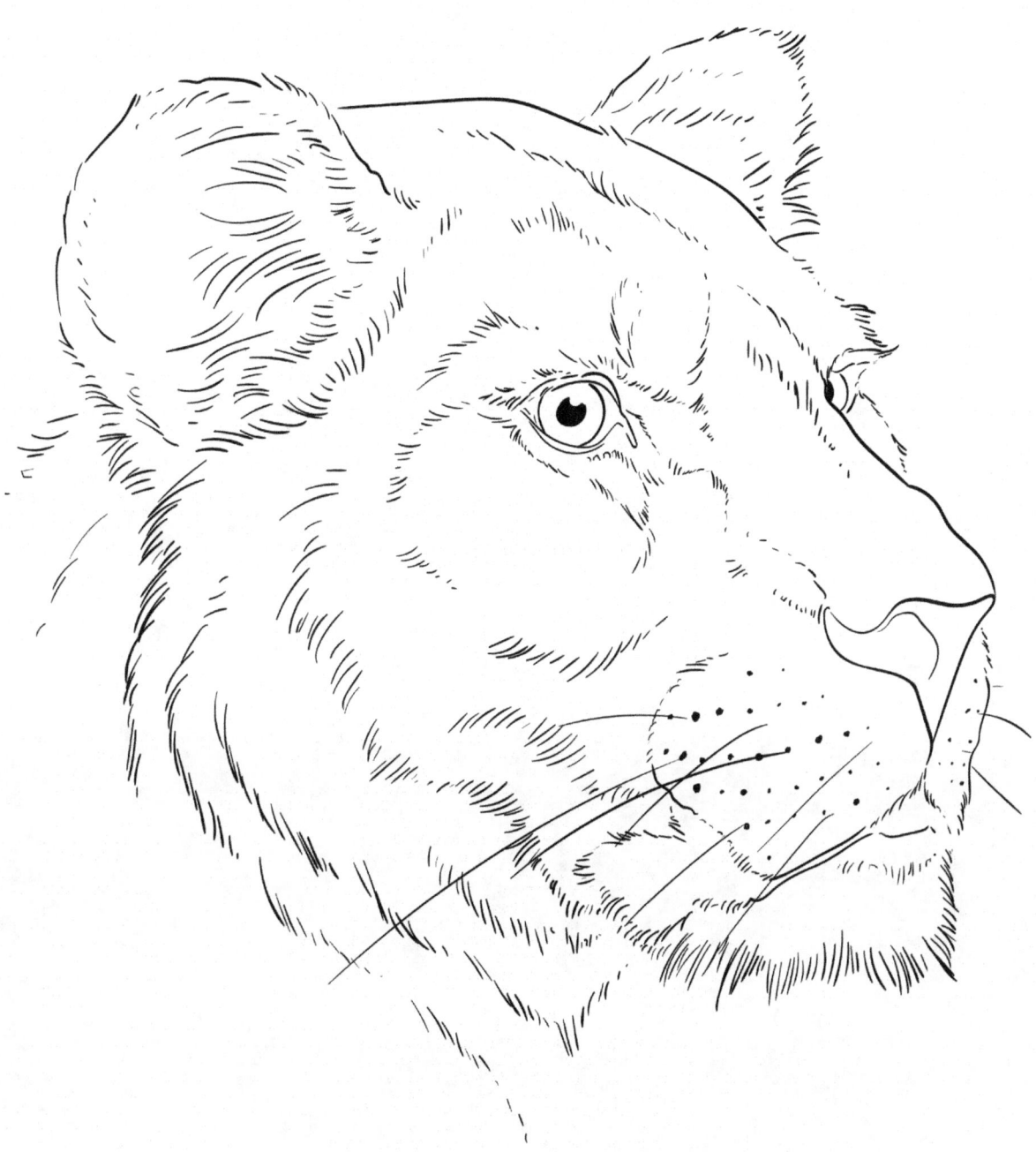

GIRAFFE

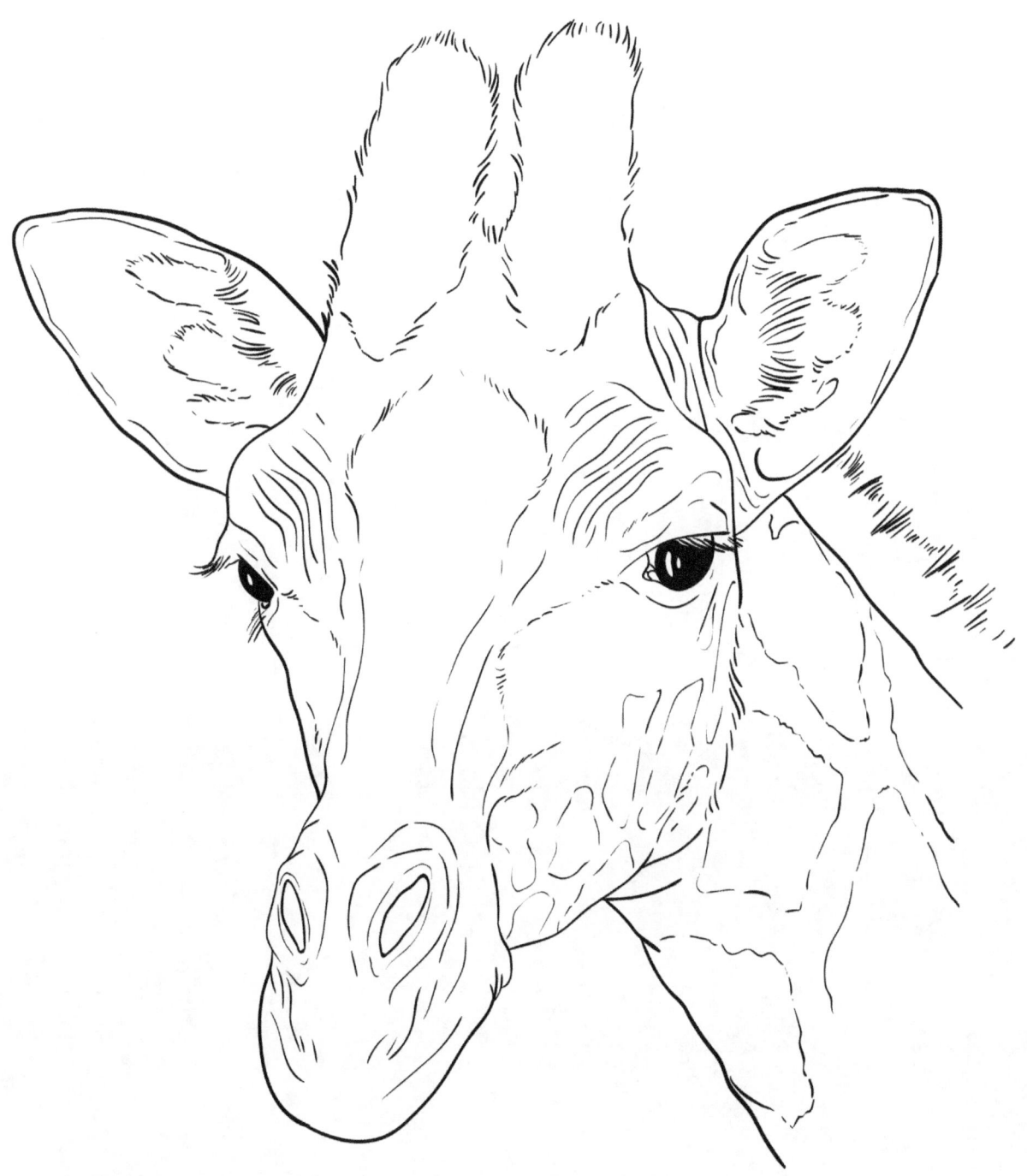

LEMUR

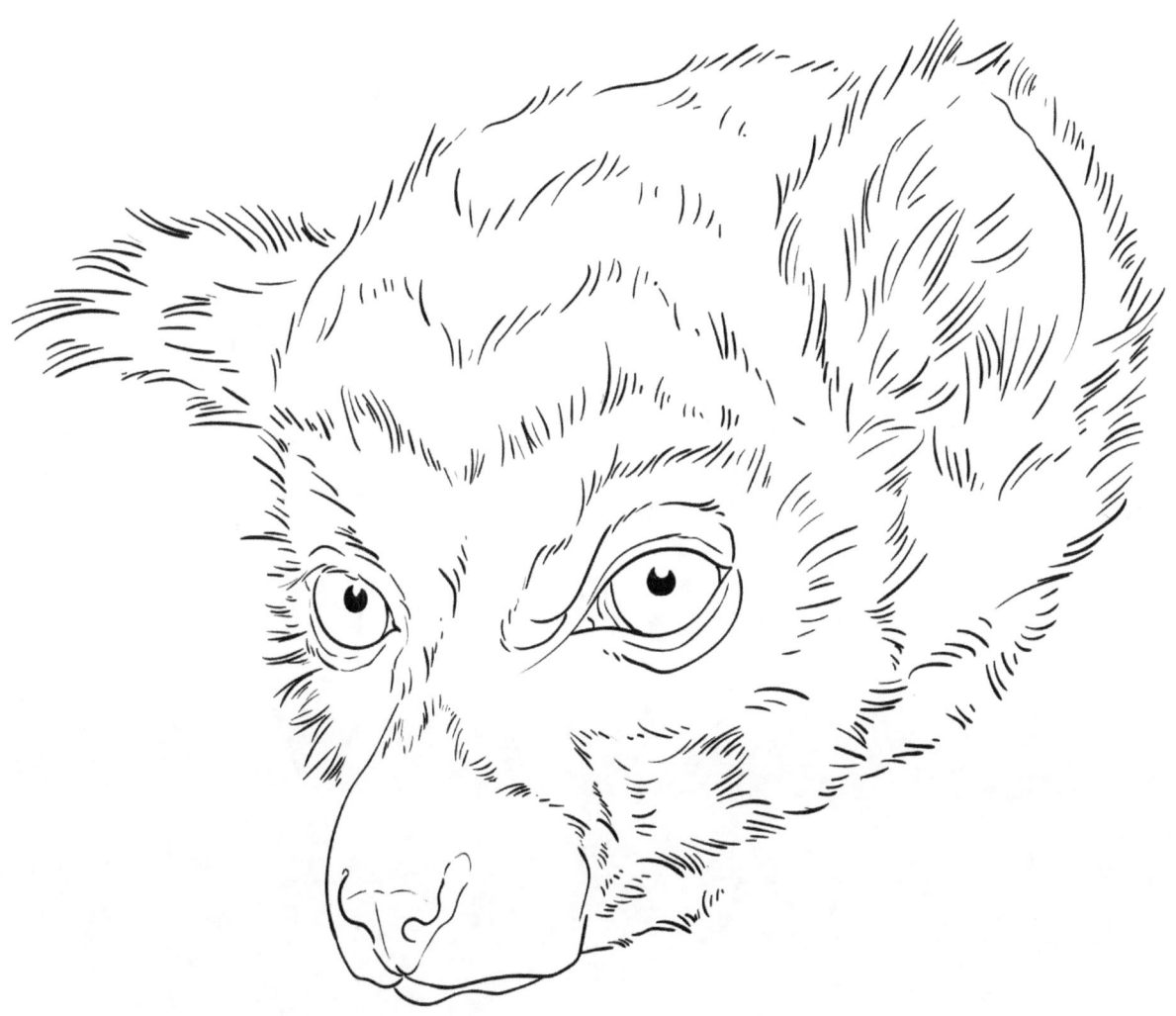

FLAMINGO

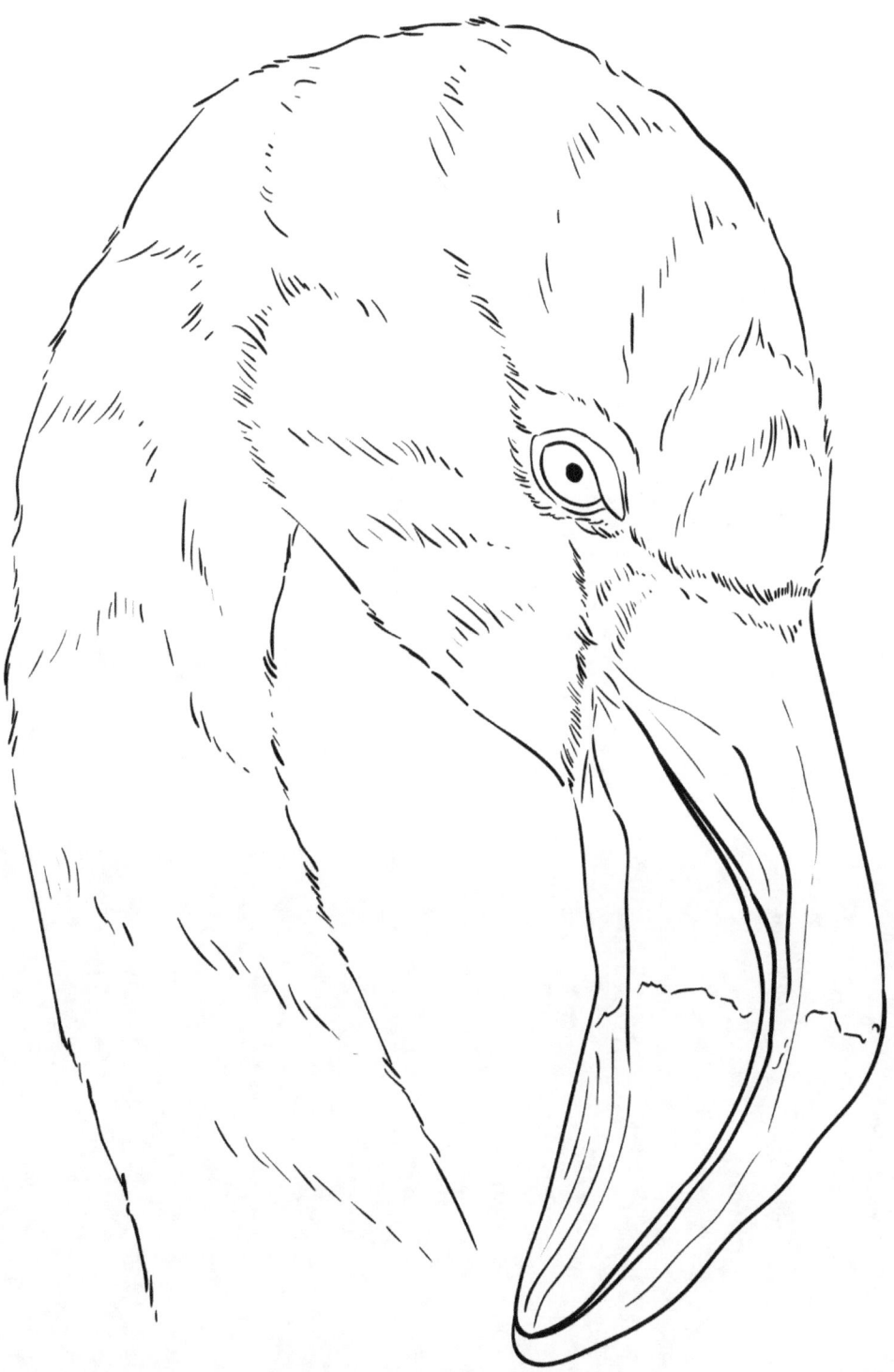

OTTER

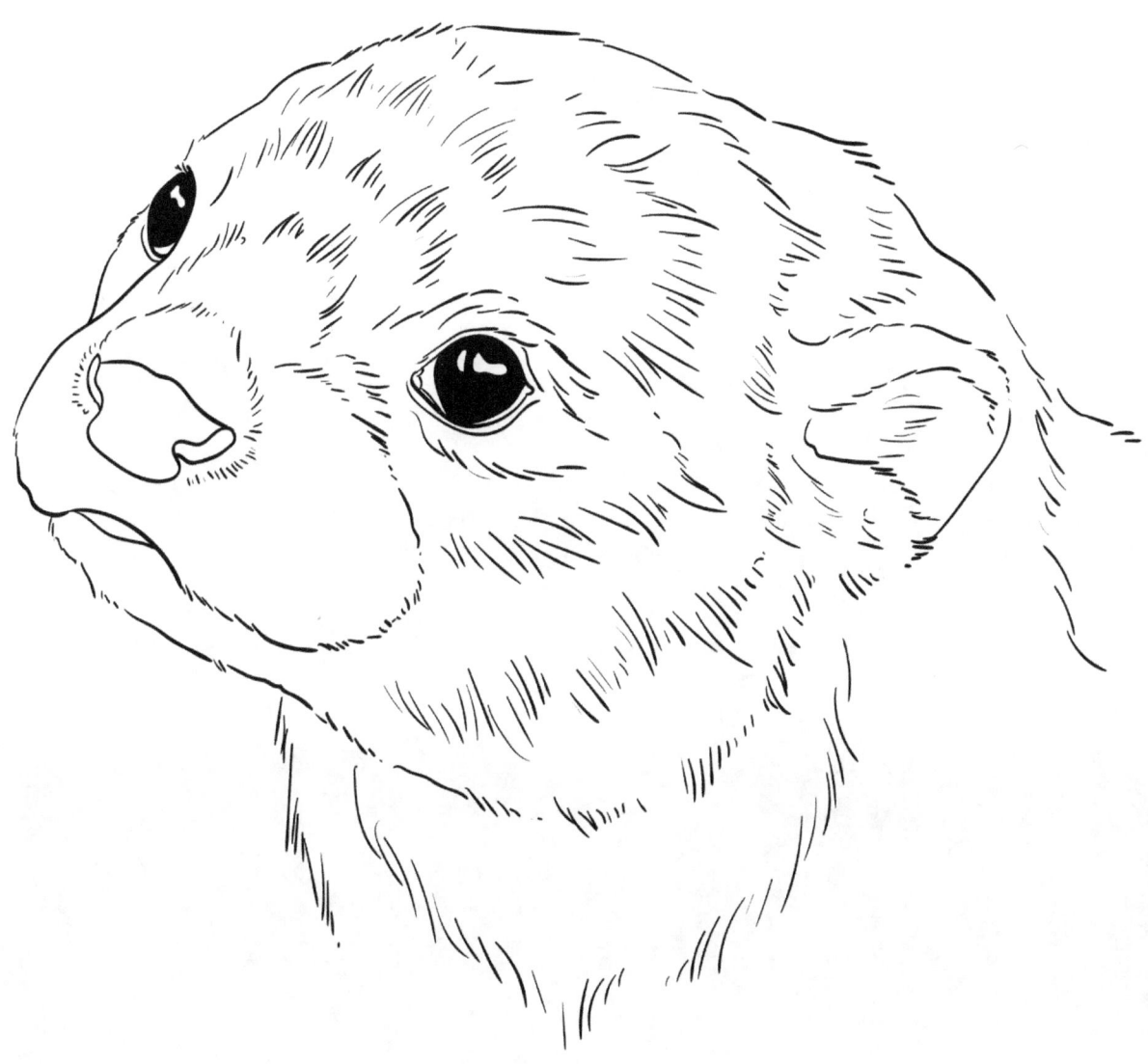

Owl

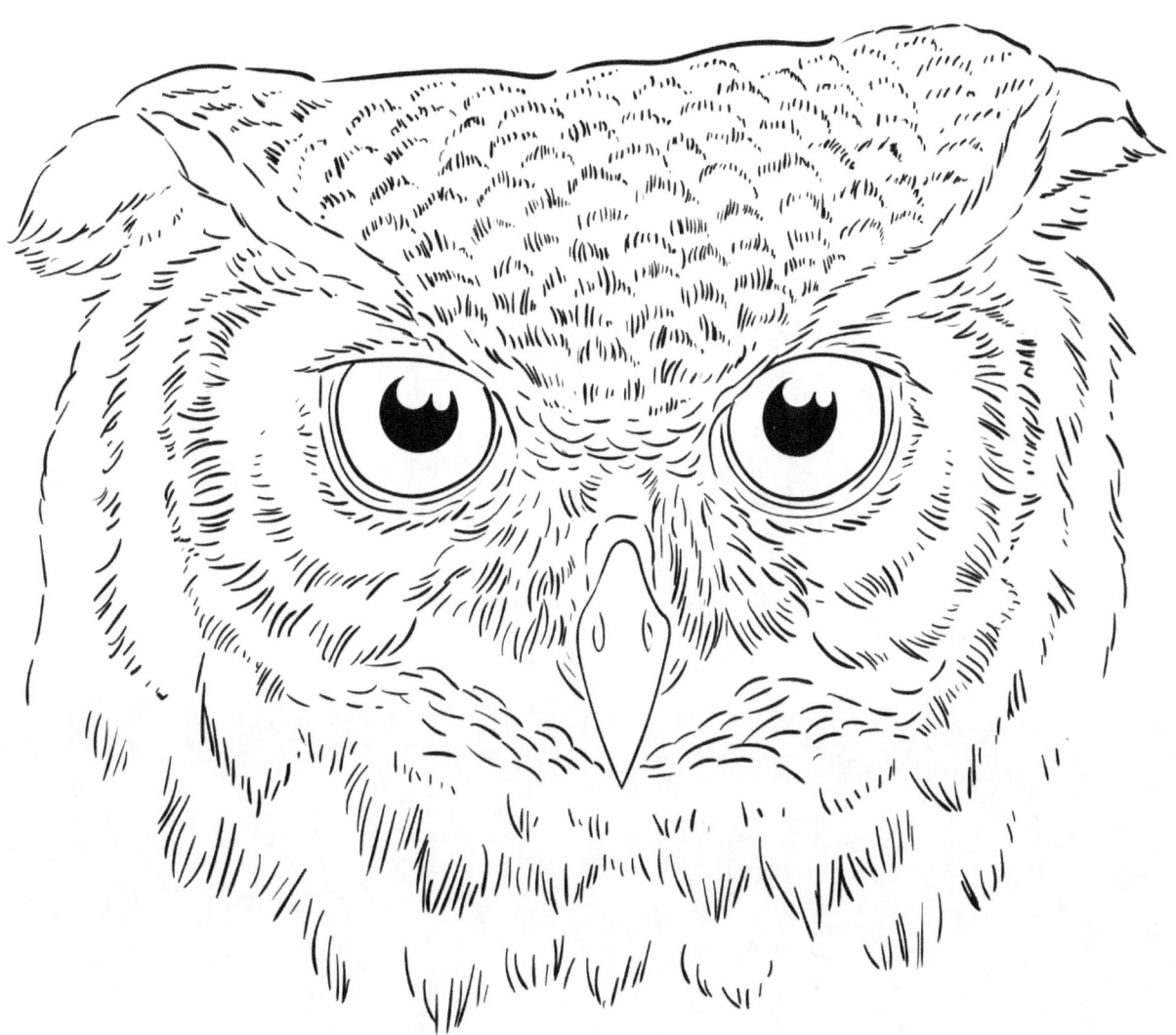

SNAKE

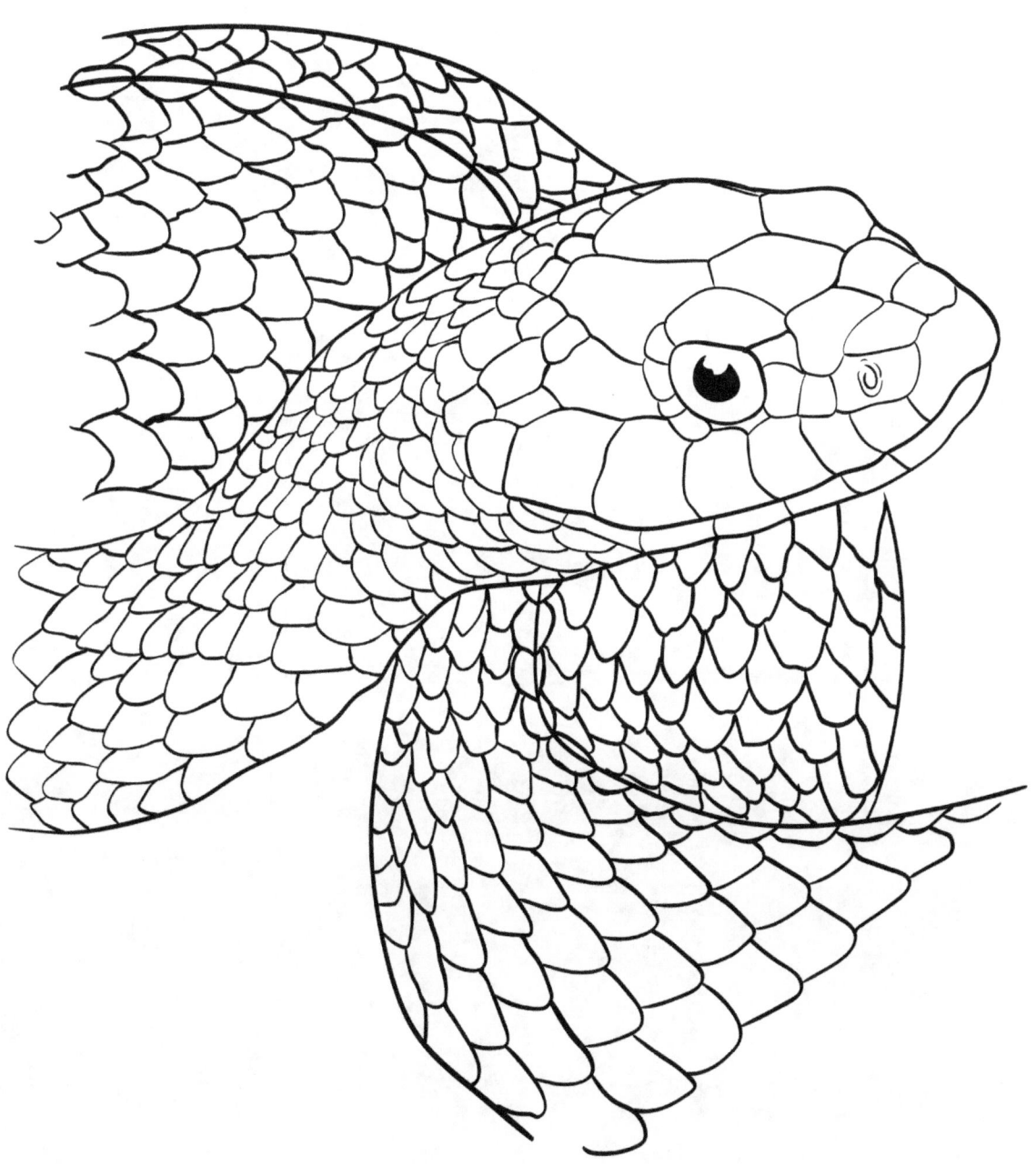

COCKEREL

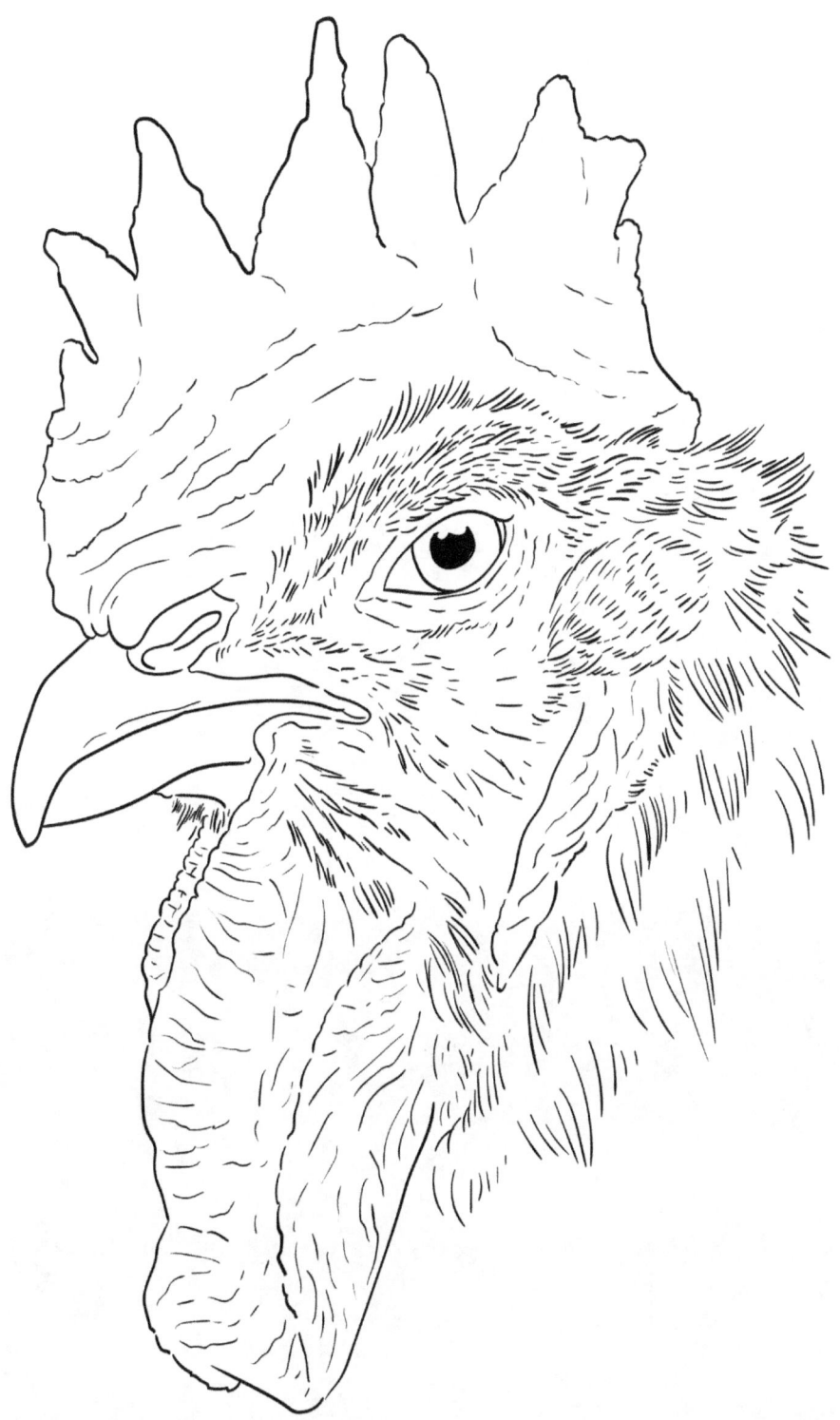

DUCK

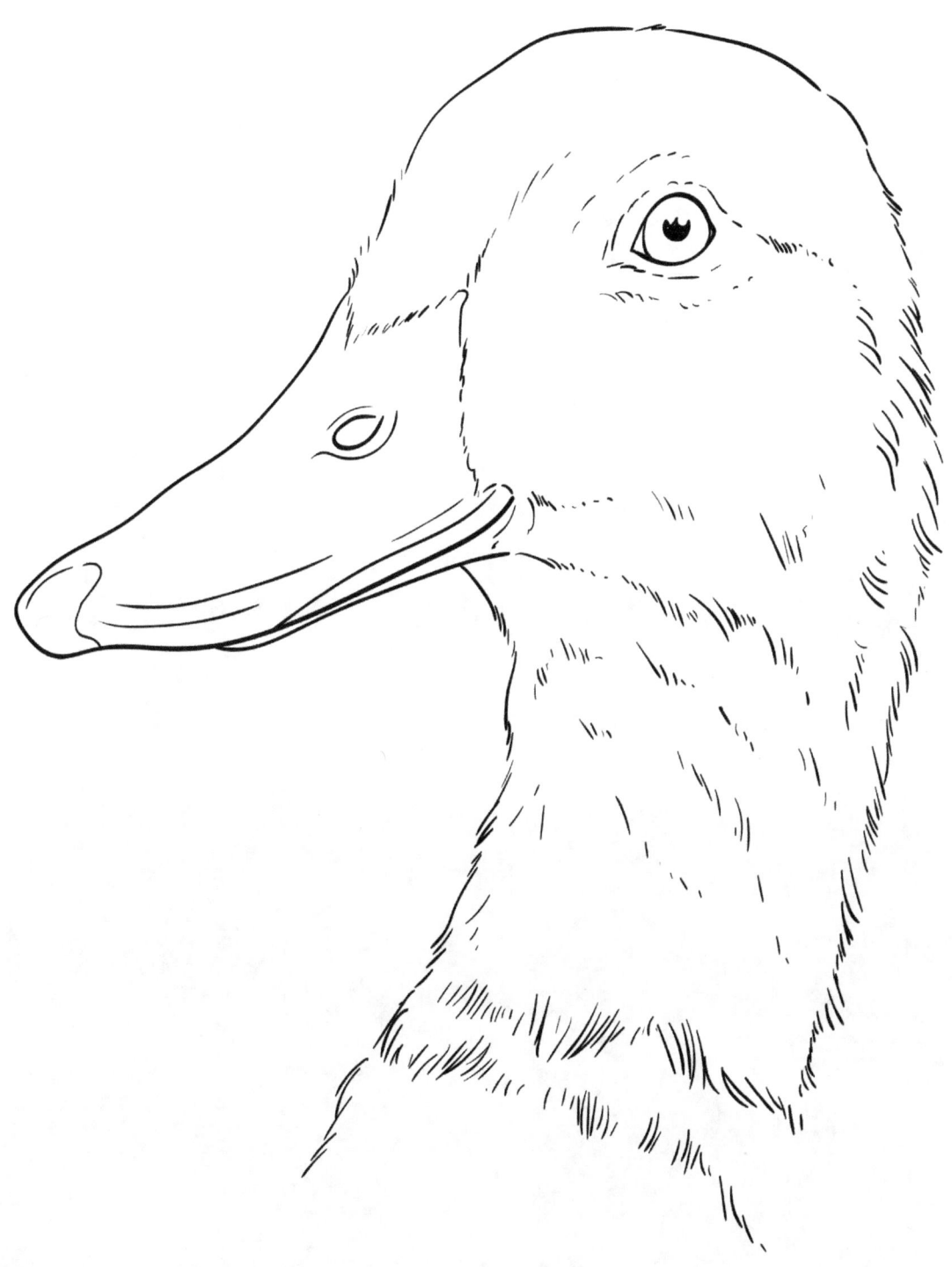

GORILLA

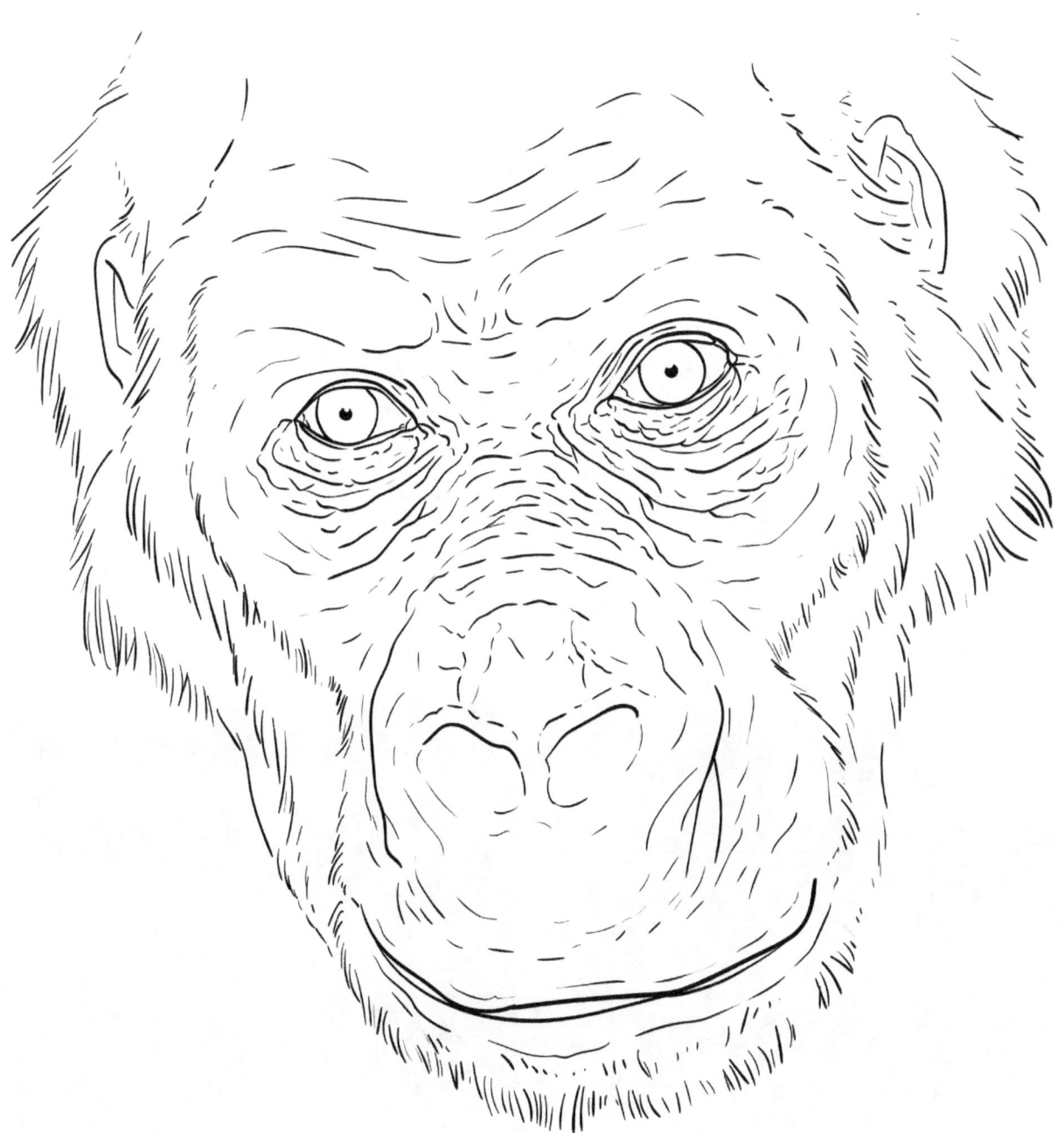

HORSE

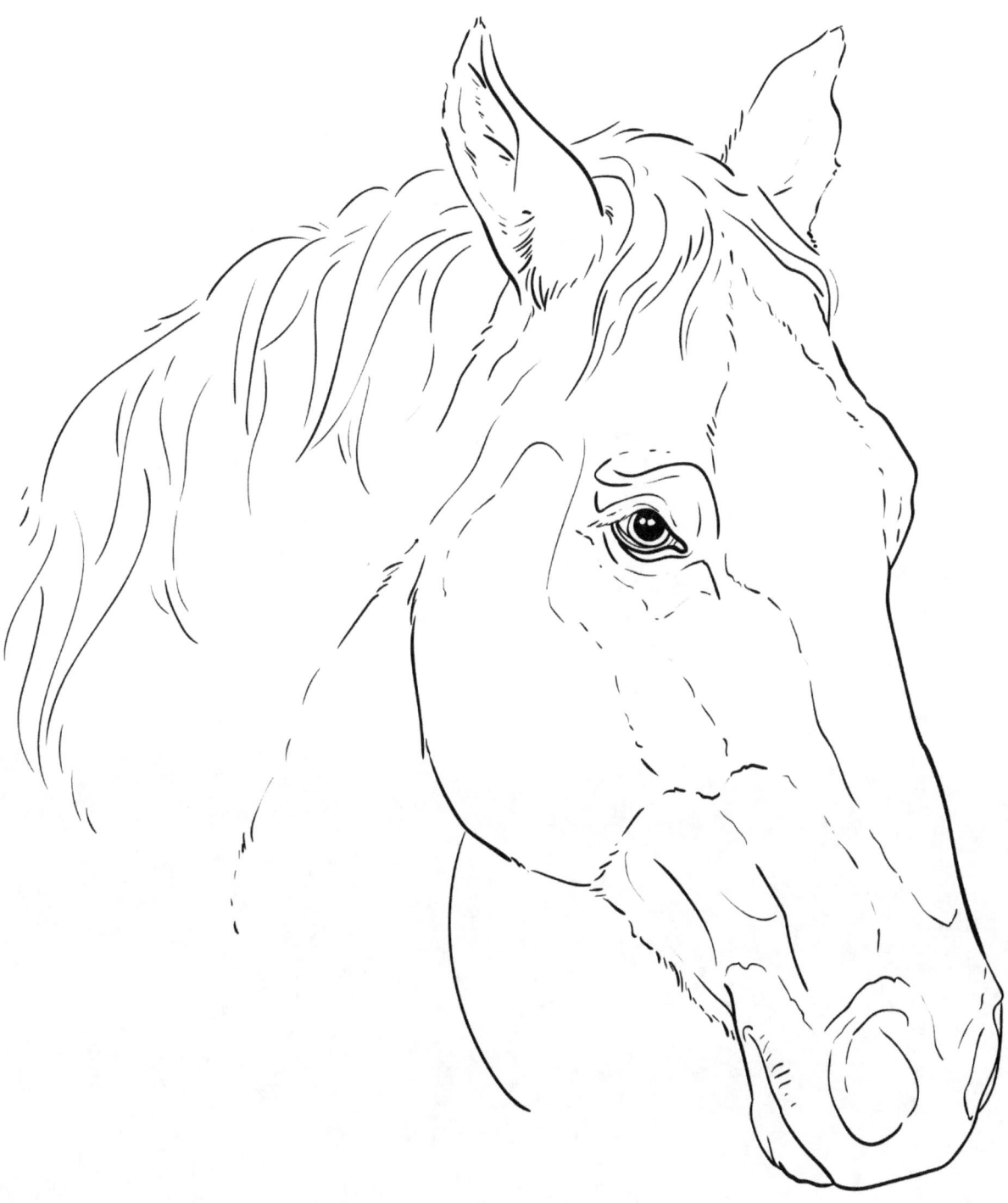

TIGER

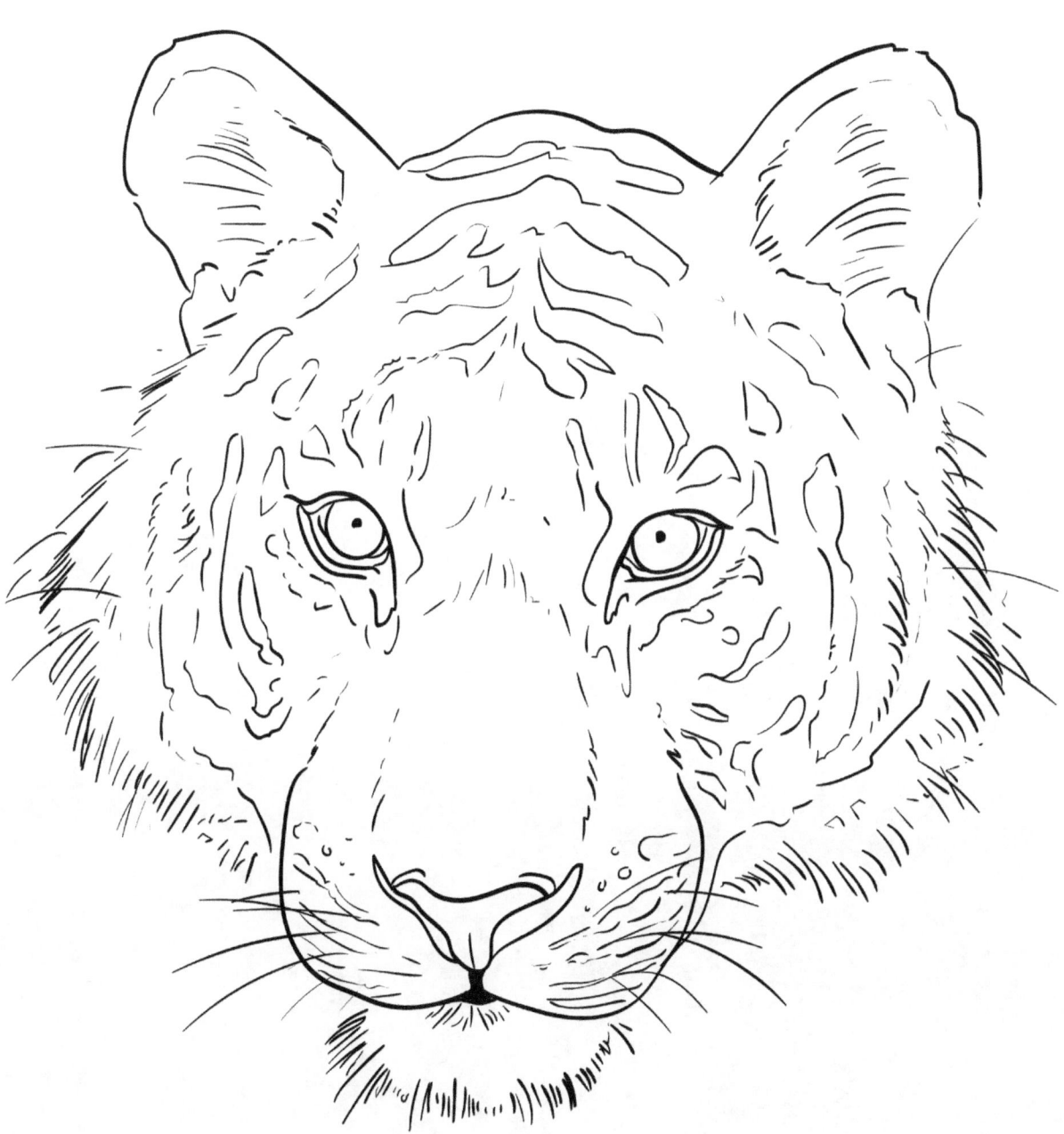

RABBIT

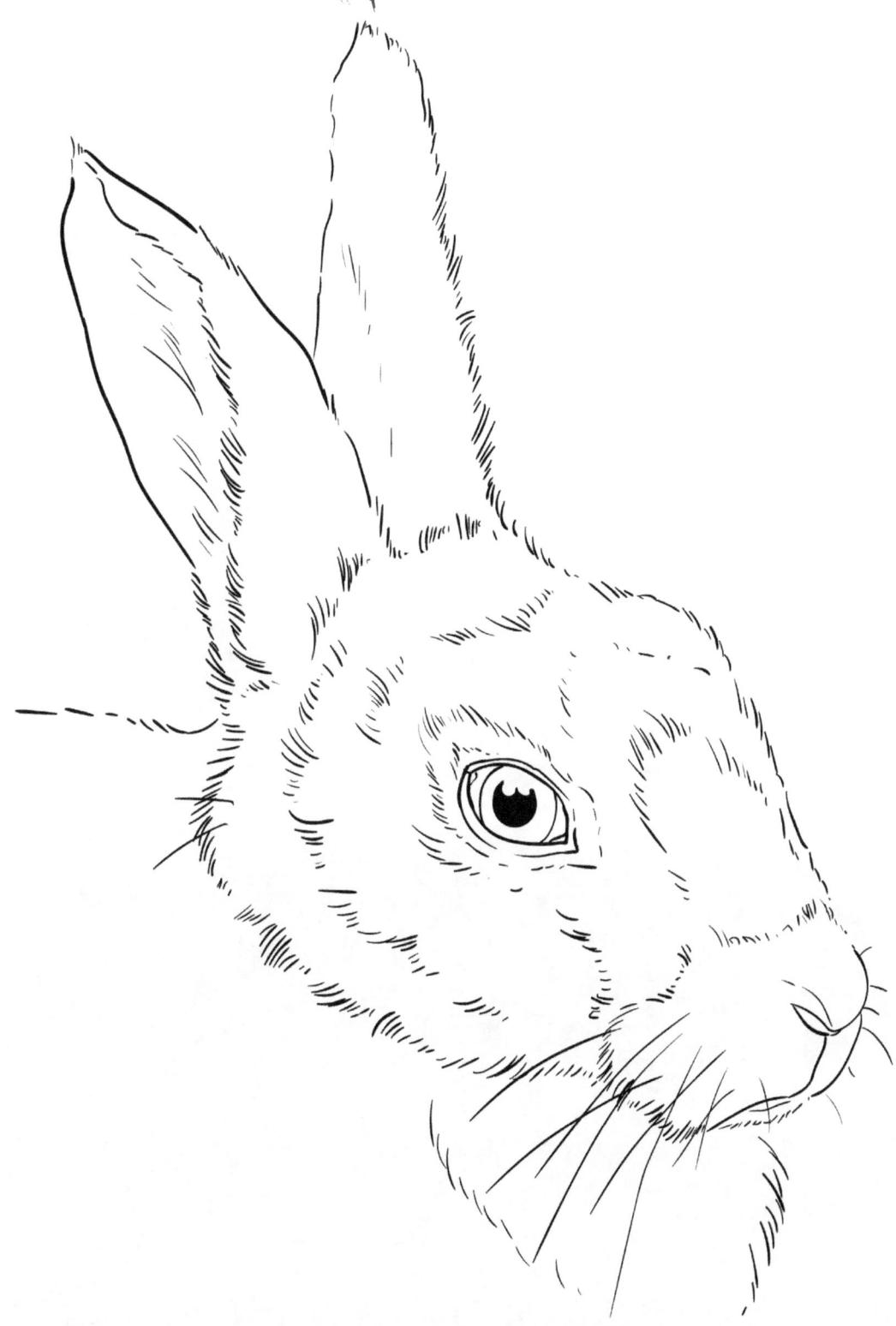

WOLF

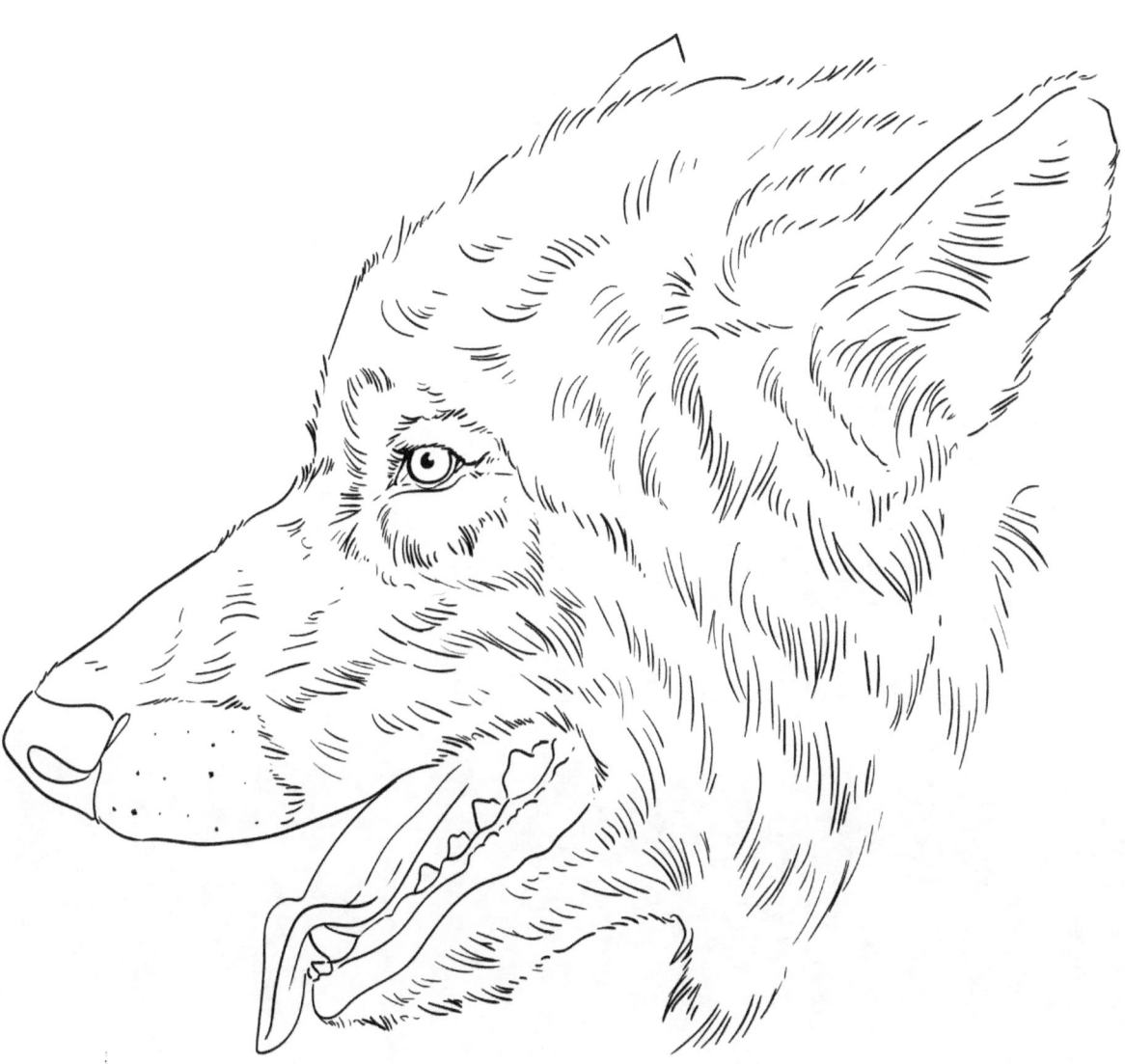

EAGLE

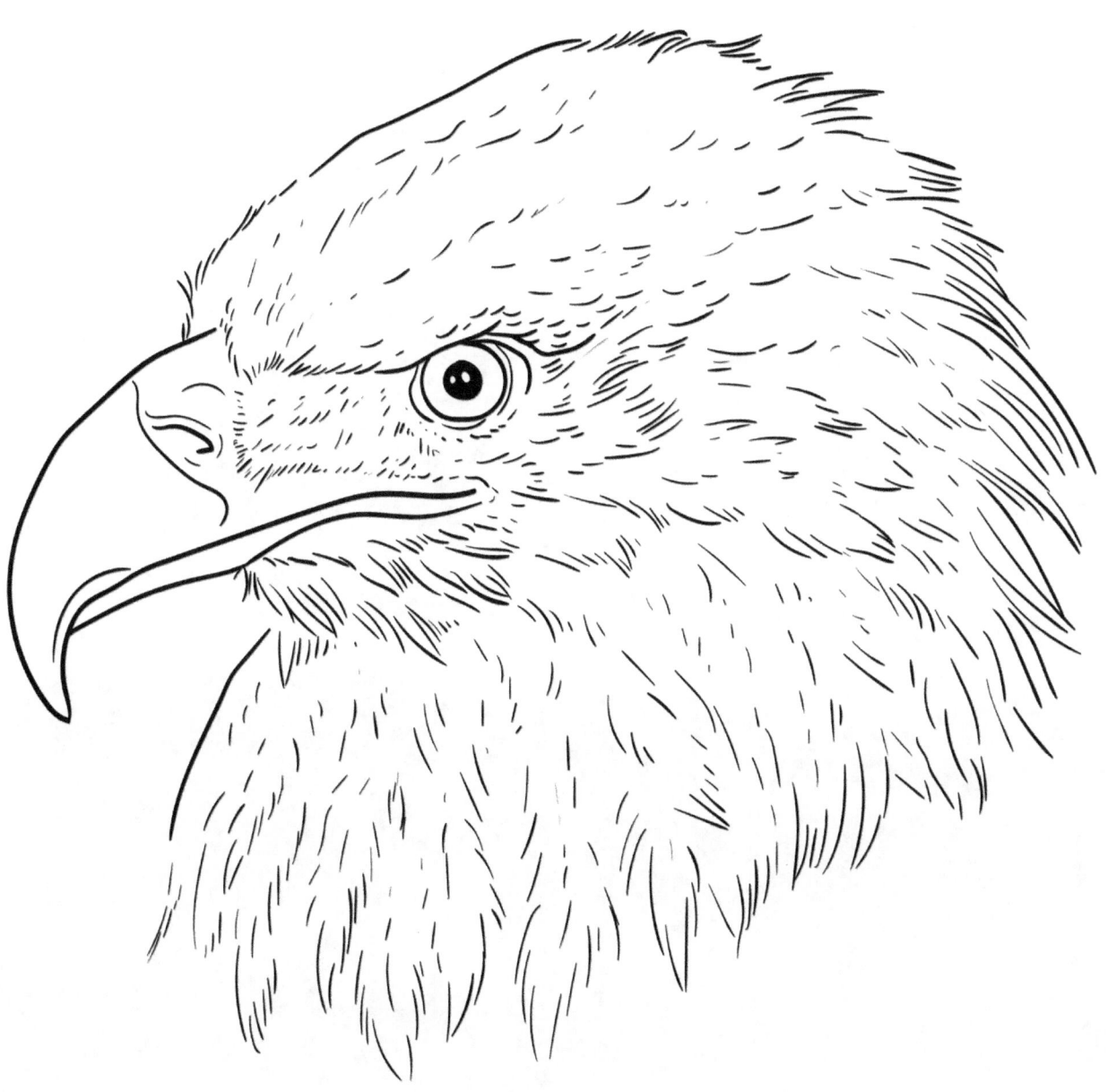

LEOPARD

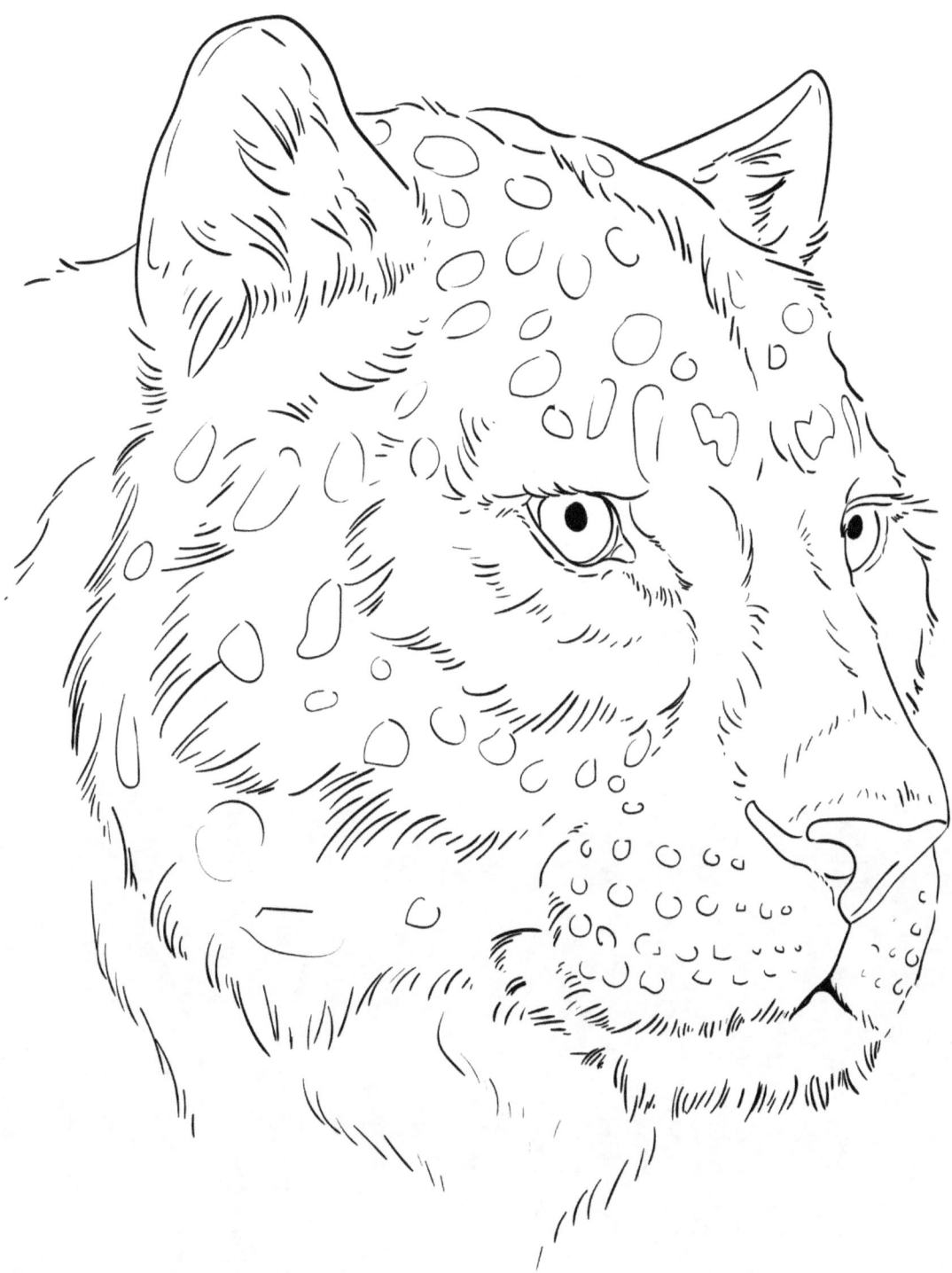

MEERKAT

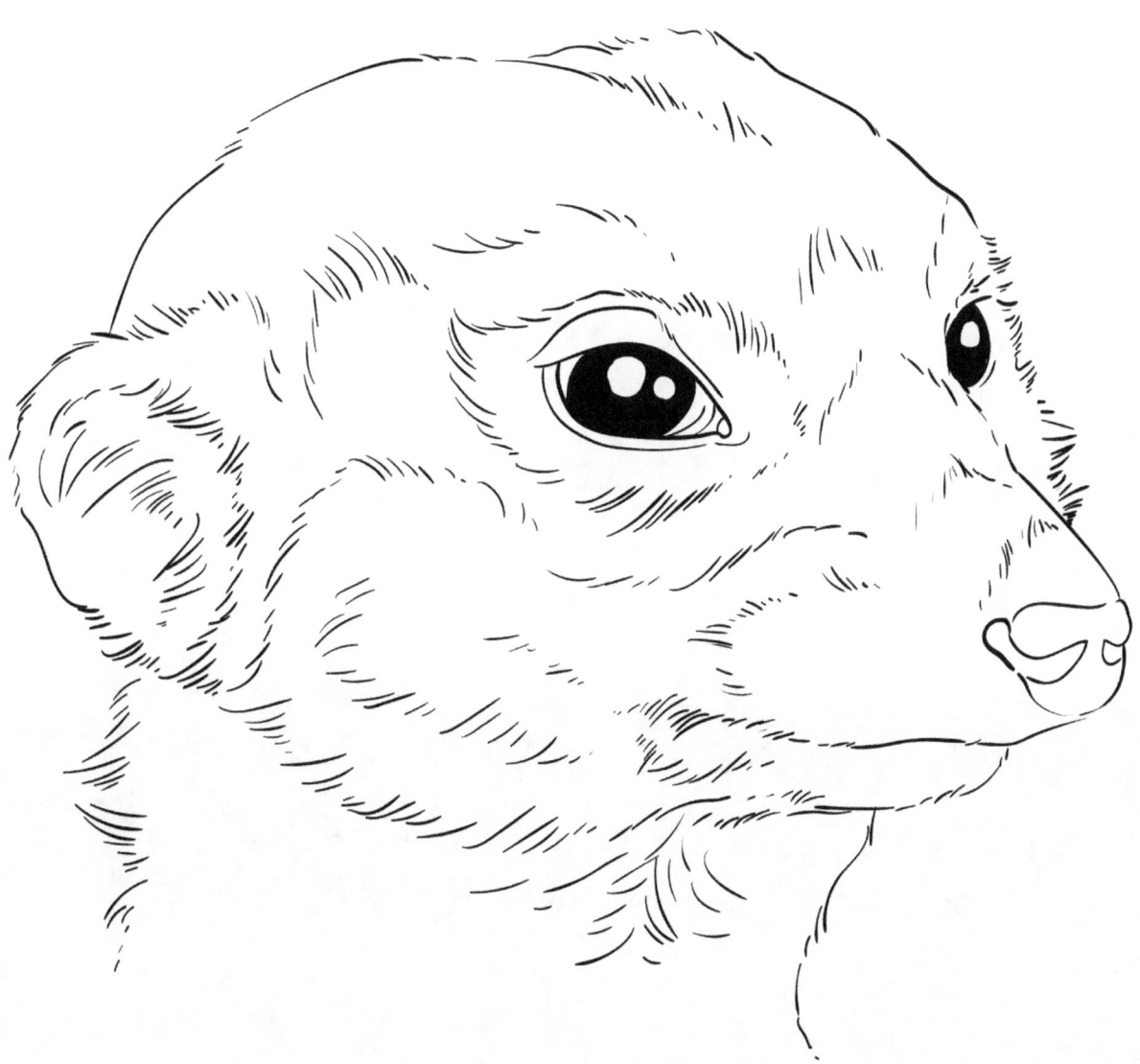

PUG

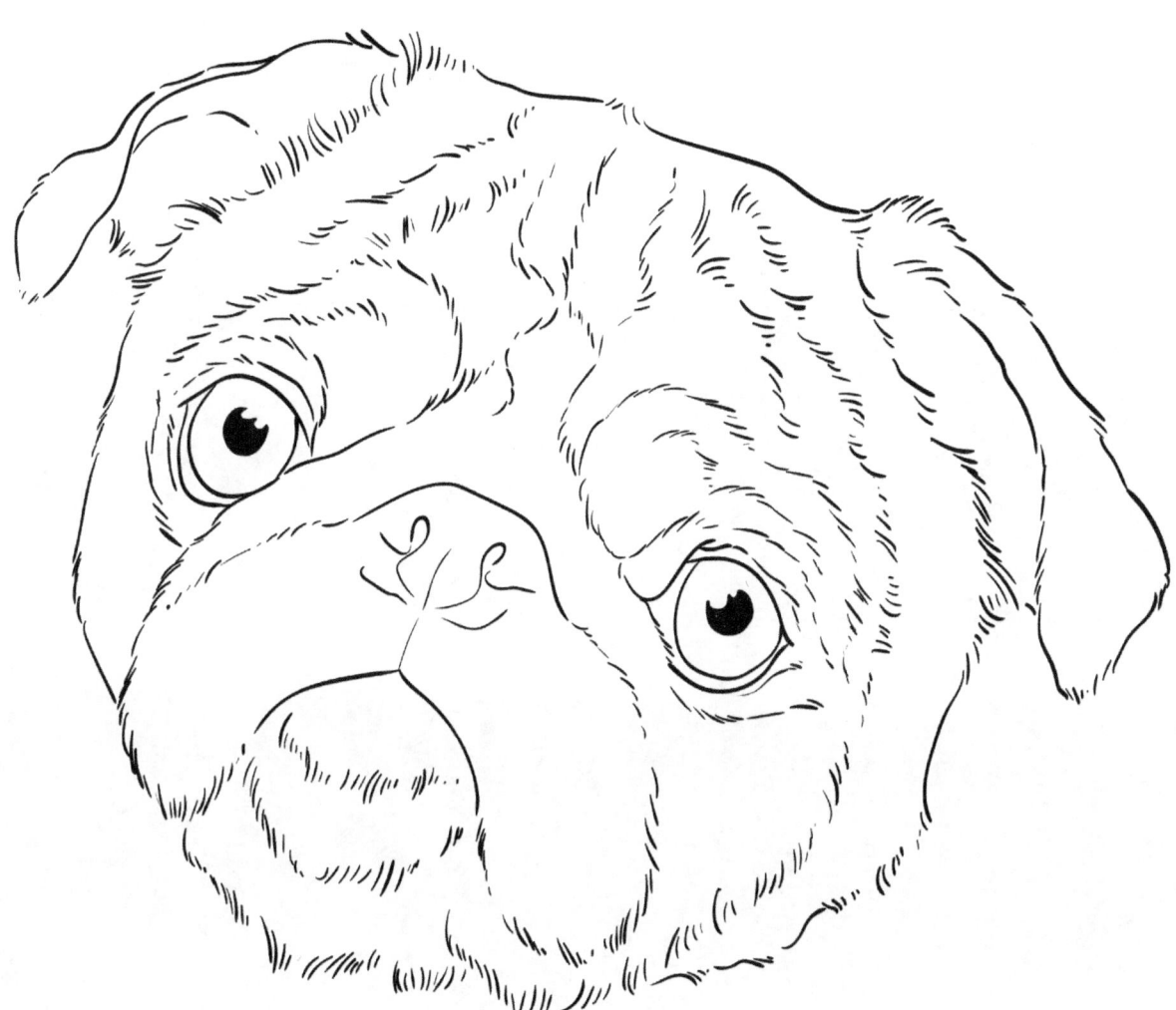

ZEBRA

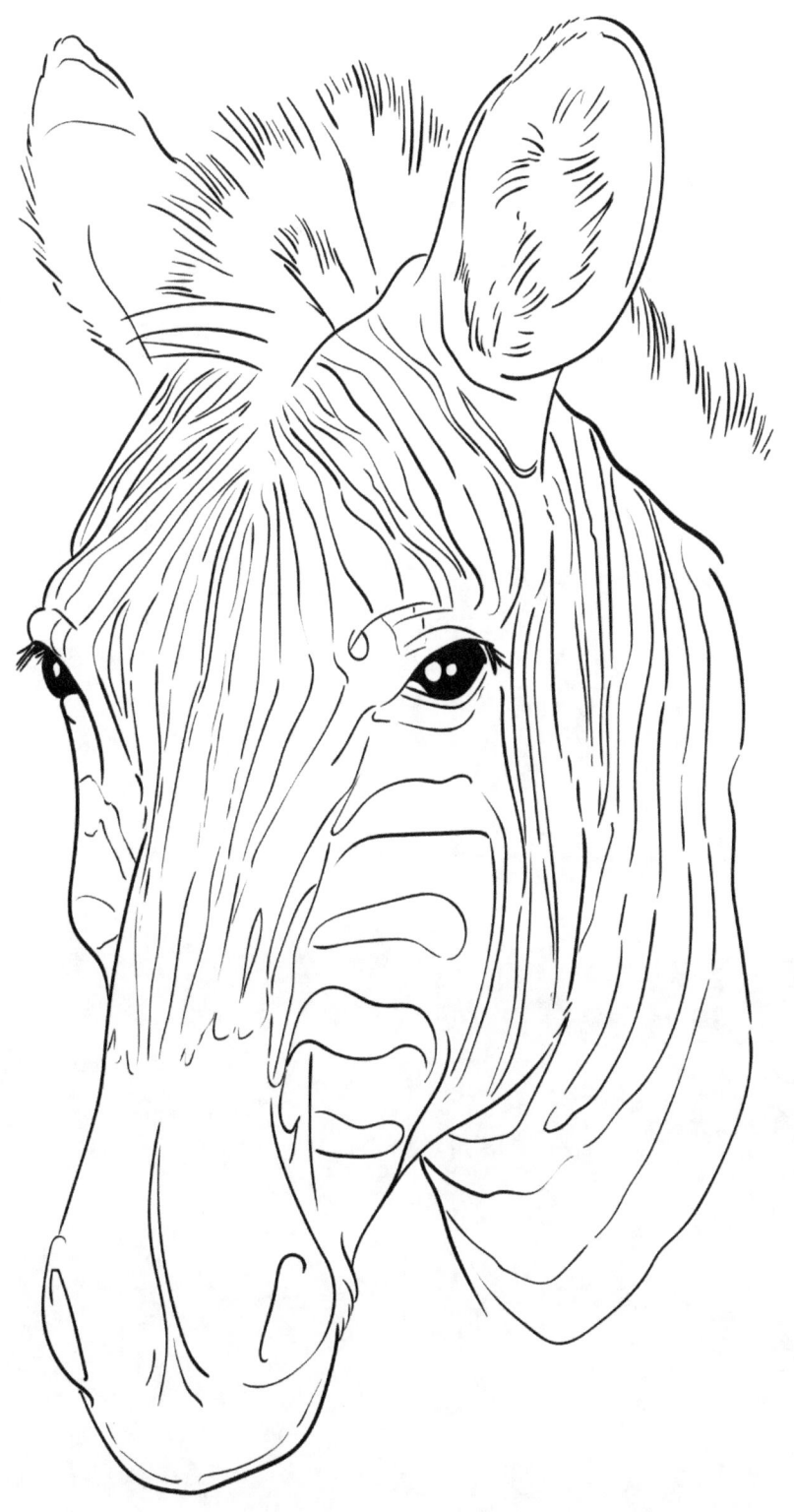

PENGUIN

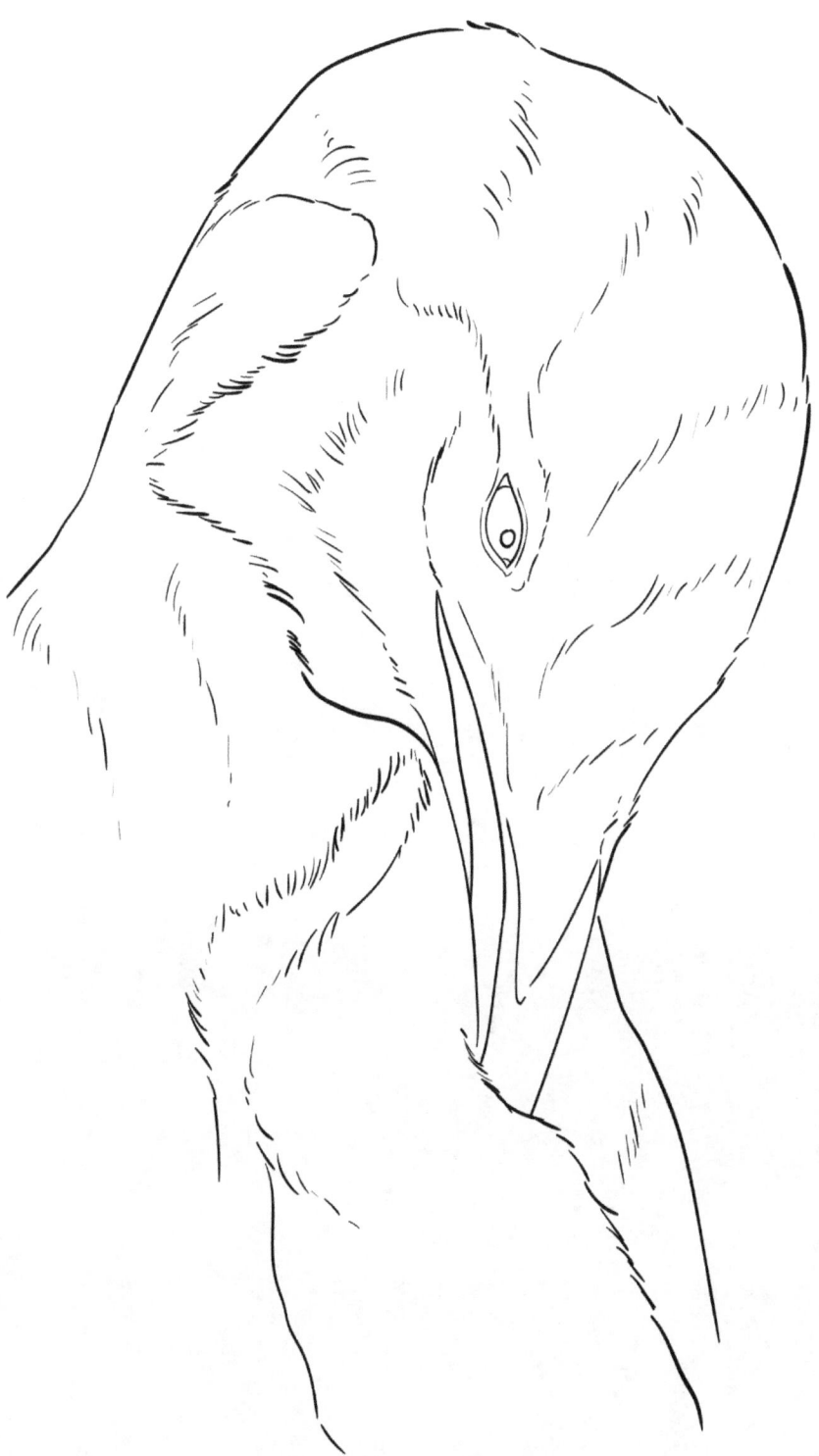